SURVEY OF LIBRARY CAFÉS

© 2007 Primary Research Group Inc.   ISBN #: 1-57440-089-4

TABLE OF CONTENTS

LIST OF TABLES

LIST OF PARTICIPANTS

Helm-Cravens Library, Western Kentucky
University
Rockwall County Library
Champaign County Library
Albertsons Library, Boise State University
Howell Carnegie Library
Scottsdale Public Library
Georgetown Public Library
James A. Michener Library, BCFL
Joseph T. Simpson Public Library
Virginia Beach Central Library
Barton County Community College Library
Salina Public Library
Clearwater Public Library
Waverly Branch Library
Kansas City Kansas Community College Library
Santa Barbara City College, Luria Library
Alameda Free Library
Mohave Community College Library (4 branches)
Horry County Memorial Library
American International College
Northcentral Technical College Library
David O. McKay Library
Gogebic Community College
University Of Detroit Mercy Dental Library
Toledo-Lucas County Public Library
Grainfield City Library
Alameda Free Public Library
Frisco Public Library
Richardson Public Library
Santa Monica Public Library
Hernando Public Library
Germantown Library
McGovern Library
Topeka and Shawnee County Public Library
Pikes Peak Library District
Wood County District Public Library
Main Library - Central Arkansas Library System
College of DuPage Library
University of Texas, Arlington

SUMMARY OF MAIN FINDINGS

Percentage of Libraries in the Sample Offering a Café, Restaurant, Mobile Food Cart or Vending Machines

A shade more than half of the libraries in the sample had a library café, and most of the rest had coffee stations or vending machines. Only 20% of the smallest libraries, those with 100,000 or fewer visitors, had a library café. Otherwise, library size was not a predictor of the tendency to have a library café; those with between 100,000 and 250,000 annual visitors were only slightly more likely to have a café than those with more than 600,000 visitors. Only one library in the sample had a full restaurant.

Only two libraries in the sample had mobile carts from which they sell beverages and snacks, while close to a third of the libraries in the sample had vending machines. Only 10% of libraries with less than 100,000 annual visitors had vending machines, as well as close to 40% of college libraries in the sample.

Annual Sales Volume for the Cafe

The mean annual sales volume of the cafes in the sample was $45,200 with a range from zero (some libraries gave away coffee and tea without charge) to $180,000. Not all libraries supplied these figures and those that have outsourced the library café were less likely to provide a figure; sales may be higher at these libraries. Sales volume grew rapidly with library size and the largest libraries averaged $138,000 in annual sales while the smallest ones averaged only $500.00.

Reasons for Opening a Cafe

Most of the libraries in the sample had started their cafes recently, generally within the past five years. Patron requests were one of the major catalysts for new café openings, and cafes often accompanied new building construction. Some librarians observed the success of cafes in bookstores and wanted to emulate the practice. Some cited outside pressure from college management. All seemed to be looking for ways to satisfy, retain and grow the patron base.

Snacks, Breakfast, Lunch and Dinner as a Percentage of Café Revenues

Snacks accounted for nearly 71% of the income of the library cafes in the sample, though lunch added a not at all negligible 20.83% of total revenue and break fast chipped in with another 8.33%. None of the café's served dinner. Interestingly, lunch accounted for twice the level of overall sales in public libraries than in college libraries, which relied more on snacks and breakfast (perhaps it's those all nighter study sessions). Only the larger libraries, however, in terms of patron base, earned any of their revenue from breakfast, and these earned approximately between 14-17% of their revenue from breakfast.

Coffee as a Percentage of Total Sales

As might be expected, sales of coffee accounted for a high percentage of sales, 38.45%. For college libraries, coffee accounted for nearly 59% of total sales and, incredibly, a median of 75% of total sales.

Particular Foods as a Percentage of Sales

Salads in this era of health consciousness chipped in only a mean of 4.5% of sales, more in the public than college libraries. All salad sales came from the larger libraries, those with more than 600,000 annual patrons. Yogurt added about 1% of annual sales and, once again, only the larger institutions sold yogurt, for which sales accounted for about 2% of total revenue. Similarly, fruit was not particularly popular, accounting for 1.42% of total sales, mostly for the larger libraries. Interestingly, however, fruit accounted for a median of 5% of the total revenues of the largest category of library, suggesting that, if offered, fruit will sell.

"Junk food" a term that we left up to the imagination of the survey participants to completely define – accounted a mean of 14.29% of sales, 17% for the public libraries which serve more children than the college libraries.

Sandwiches accounted for 5% of total sales, but for 11% of the sales of the cafes in the largest libraries, the only ones to sell sandwiches.

Cold drinks accounted for a shade more than 29% of total sales, more for public than college libraries. Baked goods accounted for 7.2%, and 10% for the college libraries. Most library cafes sold baked goods of some kind, except for the smallest libraries.

Price of the Typical Cup of Coffee

The average price of a cup of coffee in the library cafes was $1.49, perhaps reflecting the Starbuck-ization of the library café. This figure also takes in to account those libraries that gave their coffee away. The median price was $1.50. Public libraries actually charged more than college libraries, even though some public libraries gave the coffee away. The smallest libraries charge only 55 cents, on average, for a cup of coffee, while for the other libraries, the mean price ranged from $1.54 to $1.89.

Staffing the Library Cafe

Most library cafes did not have even one full time employee; however, the mean number of employees was 1.17 and one café had a staff of seven. The cafes of libraries with more than 600,000 annual patrons was 2.33. Overall, mean spending on salaries was only $13,320.

Impact of Food in the Library on Library Maintenance Costs

A shade less than 23% of the libraries in the sample said that offering food in the library led to higher library maintenance and clean up costs.   A quarter of public libraries and ten percent of public libraries believed this.

For 15.63% of the libraries, having a café led to higher carpeting, furnishing or other deco-related costs. In this case, more than 18% of college libraries had this experience but only 10% of public libraries.

Best Selling Items

Coffee was the best selling item; otherwise, most of the most popular foods items reported were from the "carb" family – muffins, scones, pastries, cookies, and crackers. Sandwiches, croissant sandwiches, wraps, pitas, salads, and soups were also mentioned, along with candy, chips, and other dessert items.

As you might expect, many libraries reported the traditional drink choices of coffee, tea, cocoa, soda, and other cold drinks as big sellers. A few reported more "upscale" expresso-based coffee drinks (lattes, etc.) and/or fruit-based drinks (smoothies) as popular choices.

Policies to Protect the Library from Food

Librarians in the sample use a variety of imaginative methods to protect the library from the inevitable food and beverage spills and mishaps. Many recommend lids on drinks at all times; others restrict all food and beverages to a particular area, and remind patrons to let librarians know about food and beverage mishaps immediately. Some ban foods that are particularly greasy or that crumble easily. Some recommend the provision of generous numbers of trash receptacles.

Workstations, Wireless Access & the Library Café

Ninety percent of the library cafes in the sample are wireless hot spots; all of the college library cafes were wireless hot spots, as were nearly 84% of the public library cafes. A quarter of the cafes had computer workstations for patrons, nearly 42% of the college library cafes and almost 16% of the public library cafes. The smallest libraries were the most likely to put workstations in the library café, perhaps reflecting a greater need to make multi tasking use of available space.

Percentage of Library Cafes with Outdoor Seating

More than 40% of the library cafes offered outdoor seating; more than 47% of public library cafes in the sample offered outdoor seating. In general, the larger libraries were more likely than the smaller libraries to offer outdoor seating in the café.

What the Café Serves

More than fifty percent of the library cafes serve muffins, though only a bit less than 31% served croissants, and about 40% served bagels. More than 28% served sandwiches and close to 13% serve hot sandwiches. All of the libraries that served hot sandwiches were public libraries and all had more than 250,000 patrons per year.

Only 5.13% of the libraries in the sample served hamburgers, all libraries with more than 600,000 patrons per year.

About 18% of the libraries in the sample served soup. Only 5.13% served main dinner entrees. More than 20% served yogurt while only 5.13% served troublesome popcorn.

Did the Library Café Help to Increase Patron Traffic?

Nearly two thirds of the libraries in the sample believed that their library café had helped them to increase the number of patrons visiting the library. Nearly 73% of college libraries and close to 59% of public libraries felt this way. Close to 90% of the libraries surveyed felt that the addition of the café had led to patrons spending more time in the library. All of the public libraries felt this way, as did about 73% of the college libraries. All of the libraries that felt otherwise were very small libraries with less than 100,000 visitors per year.

Vending Machines in the Library

Close to 65% of the libraries in the sample had vending machines, with an average of only about three vending machines per library. The largest libraries, with 100,000 or fewer visitors, averaged 1.4 vending machines per library, while the larger libraries, with 601,000 or more visitors, averaged 4.14 vending machines per library.

Mobile Food Carts & Kiosks for the Library

None of the libraries in the sample had mobile kiosks or carts to serve food in out of the way places.

Catering Library Functions

More than 34% of the cafes in the sample cater library functions. Only about 9.1% of college library cafes did so, while half of public library cafes catered library functions. In general, the larger the library, the more likely is the café to cater library functions.

Advice to those Contemplating the Start up or Revision of a Library Cafe

The overwhelming majority of the libraries in the sample that have a café, more than 93%, advise libraries that do not have a café to start one. More than half, however, suggest inviting in a franchise to run it, while 16% suggest that the library itself run the café and nearly 26% suggest using the college food service provider. The college food service provider is the café manager of choice for more than 58% of the college libraries in the sample, while 25% of them prefer an outside franchise. More than seventy percent of public libraries prefer using an outside franchise while a bit more than 22% suggest that the library run the café itself.

DIMENSIONS OF THE SAMPLE

Table A   Library Participants

Is your library academic or public?	ACADEMIC	PUBLIC
	34.21%	65.79%

Table B   Mean, Median, Minimum and Maximum Number of Visitors to the Library in the Past Year

Approximately how many visitors did the library have in the past year?	MEAN	MEDIAN	MINIMUM	MAXIMUM
	482,406.06	263,500.00	400.00	2,150,000.00

Table C   Mean, Median, Minimum and Maximum Number of Visitors to the Library in the Past Year, Broken Out by Type of Library

TYPE OF LIBRARY	MEAN	MEDIAN	MINIMUM	MAXIMUM
College Library	315,363.92	87,500.00	500.00	1,841,000.00
Public Library	498,449.48	312,000.00	400.00	2,000,000.00

Table D   Mean, Median, Minimum and Maximum Number of Visitors to the Library in the Past Year, Broken Out by Number of Annual Visitors to the Library

ANNUAL VISITORS TO THE LIBRARY	MEAN	MEDIAN	MINIMUM	MAXIMUM
100,000 or fewer	25,547.50	21,250.00	400.00	70,000.00
100,001 - 250,000	173,375.00	169,000.00	104,000.00	250,000.00
250,001 - 600,000	347,673.38	326,000.00	258,000.00	554,387.00
601,000 or more	1,202,903.90	1,026,376.00	626,748.00	2,150,000.00

CHAPTER 1: SCOPE OF FOOD SERVICE OPERATIONS

Table 1 - 1   Percentage of Libraries that Have a Cafe

Does your library have a café?	YES	NO
	51.28%	48.72%

Table 1 - 2   Percentage of Libraries that Have a Cafe, Broken Out by Type of Library

TYPE OF LIBRARY	YES	NO
College Library	53.85%	46.15%
Public Library	48.00%	52.00%

Table 1 - 3   Percentage of Libraries that Have a Cafe, Broken Out by Number of Annual Visitors to the Library

ANNUAL VISITORS TO THE LIBRARY	YES	NO
100,000 or fewer	20.00%	80.00%
100,001 - 250,000	55.56%	44.44%
250,001 - 600,000	62.50%	37.50%
601,000 or more	60.00%	40.00%

Table 1 - 4   Percentage of Libraries that Have a Restaurant

Does your library have a restaurant?	YES	NO
	2.56%	97.44%

Table 1 - 5   Percentage of Libraries that Have a Restaurant, Broken Out by Type of Library

TYPE OF LIBRARY	YES	NO
College Library	0.00%	100.00%
Public Library	4.00%	96.00%

Table 1 - 6   Percentage of Libraries that Have a Restaurant, Broken Out by Number of Annual Visitors to the Library

ANNUAL VISITORS TO THE LIBRARY	YES	NO
100,000 or fewer	0.00%	100.00%
100,001 - 250,000	0.00%	100.00%
250,001 - 600,000	0.00%	100.00%
601,000 or more	10.00%	90.00%

Table 1 - 7   Percentage of Libraries that Have a Mobile Cart

Does your library have a mobile cart?	YES	NO
	5.13%	94.87%

Table 1 - 8   Percentage of Libraries that Have a Mobile Cart, Broken Out by Type of Library

TYPE OF LIBRARY	YES	NO
College Library	7.69%	92.31%
Public Library	4.00%	96.00%

Table 1 - 9   Percentage of Libraries that Have a Mobile Cart, Broken Out by Number of Annual Visitors to the Library

ANNUAL VISITORS TO THE LIBRARY	YES	NO
100,000 or fewer	10.00%	90.00%
100,001 - 250,000	0.00%	100.00%
250,001 - 600,000	12.50%	87.50%
601,000 or more	0.00%	100.00%

Table 1 - 10   Percentage of Libraries that Have Vending Machines

Does your library have vending machines?	YES	NO
	30.77%	69.23%

Table 1 - 11   Percentage of Libraries that Have Vending Machines, Broken Out by Type of Library

TYPE OF LIBRARY	YES	NO
College Library	38.46%	61.54%
Public Library	28.00%	72.00%

Table 1 - 12   Percentage of Libraries that Have Vending Machines, Broken Out by Number of Annual Visitors to the Library

ANNUAL VISITORS TO THE LIBRARY	YES	NO
100,000 or fewer	10.00%	90.00%
100,001 - 250,000	44.44%	55.56%
250,001 - 600,000	37.50%	62.50%
601,000 or more	30.00%	70.00%

Table 1 - 13   Mean, Median, Minimum and Maximum of Total Sales Volume in the Past Year (Calendar or Fiscal) for Cafes in the Library

What was the total sales volume in the past year (calendar or fiscal) for cafes in the library?	MEAN	MEDIAN	MINIMUM	MAXIMUM
	45,200.00	17,300.00	0.00	180,000.00

Table 1 - 14   Mean, Median, Minimum and Maximum of Total Sales Volume in the Past Year (Calendar or Fiscal) for Cafes in the Library, Broken Out by Type of Library

TYPE OF LIBRARY	MEAN	MEDIAN	MINIMUM	MAXIMUM
College Library	46,500.00	3,000.00	0.00	180,000.00
Public Library	43,900.00	35,000.00	9,600.00	96,000.00

Table 1 - 15   Mean, Median, Minimum and Maximum of Total Sales Volume in the Past Year (Calendar or Fiscal) for Cafes in the Library, Broken Out by Number of Annual Visitors to the Library

ANNUAL VISITORS TO THE LIBRARY	MEAN	MEDIAN	MINIMUM	MAXIMUM
100,000 or fewer	500.00	500.00	0.00	1,000.00
100,001 - 250,000	15,000.00	15,000.00	5,000.00	25,000.00
250,001 - 600,000	27,300.00	27,300.00	9,600.00	45,000.00
601,000 or more	138,000.00	138,000.00	96,000.00	180,000.00

CHAPTER 2: ORIGIN AND MANAGMENT OF FOOD SERVICE OPERATIONS

We asked the libraries in the sample when and why they started their library cafes. Most had been stared within the past five years. The responses of the libraries are listed next to the bullets below:

When and Why Libraries Started Their Cafés or Restaurants

- The cafe was opened in 2003
- Cooperation with University Food Services. The library doesn't manage any of it financially, so don't know numbers above.
- In 2004, when the Youth area was remodeled, a 'cafe' area with 2 vending machines was added. (Hot and cold drinks only - no food).
- Experimented temporarily with a coffee cafe in one branch library two years ago. Vendor had other business issues and pulled out. We learned the public liked the cafe!
- Cafe started in late January, 2007 when library opened new building - moved from old building to new building, single location
- Cafe was included in new building construction. Public interest led to its existence. Staffing has been unavailable so it is a nice round with vending machines that are outsourced plus a coffee service vending machine which is in the negative by approx $400. Admin has chosen to continue the service
- Vending machines were installed in March 2004 as part of a renovation project. We did not feel we had space available to allocate for a cafe and felt the vending machines would be an alternative to the cafe.
- We only opened the Coffee Shop in February 2007. We have been working to get this started, ever since the Barnes & Noble moved in down the street with their coffee shop.
- Just started about 3 months ago
- We started in 2005. We were doing a renovation, which created an expanded lobby space (17'x40'). We brainstormed on the best use of the space and came up with the concept of coffee shop and art gallery.
- spring 2005   to see if the library could attract more visitors
- August 2006. We saw a need to revitalize the library and this was a model used in other libraries. The administration supported the idea and helped to identify funding. It was done in conjunction with remodeling the computer lab area too.
- Cafe opened about a 1 1/2 months after new library opened. Community Needs Assessment and public input requested cafe or some time of food service in the library.
- The library started offering free coffee & tea in 2005. Staff were sold because this move would increase foot traffic, which is what is needed.
- The Library Friends group handles the vending machines at the one location that we have them at. This is the only money producing operation that we have. Most food that is consumed in the library is the food brought in by patrons or on special occasions (National Library Week, birthdays, anniversaries, grand openings, groundbreakings, programs, etc) where the food is supplied by the Friends, the Library, or the entity providing the program.
- 4 Years ago. We moved the vending machines from an out-of-the-way location to prime real estate on the main floor next to the main entrance. We saw immediate positive response from students and have since expanded twice.
- 2005 Wanted to see if the students would like it.
- 2002 Enhance Patron Services and Experience. Convenience.
- Library cafe was started in Dec 2006 when a new Library was opened. It was a project of the Friends of the Library and run solely by volunteers. In a survey of patrons, a cafe was

the one item most wanted in the new building.

- With the opening of the new main library
- Customer surveys. Observation of competition (bookstores).
- Part of the design of new Main Library, based on community feedback. Cafe is leased to a restaurant, so money is not part of library revenue.
- The library put in vending machines in the cafe area at its latest renovation about four years ago. It was to give our patrons a place to relax and enjoy their food in the library.
- Cafe started this past year .... primarily as a result of pressure from the city.
- August 2006 -- we moved to a new library building, and the cafe/coffee bar was part of the building plan. It was seen as a good PR move for the college, and the library staff was in favor.
- 2000 - Restaurant was added when we remodeled and expanded our existing building. Demand from the public motivated the addition.
- About five years ago, requests from patrons
- We began providing coffee and hot tea in our Atrium in 2003. Sales are by donation. No library funds are used for this service.
- Private vendor has been part of the Cox Creative Center, housing a used bookstore, art galleries and meeting space.
- The cafe has been open for 4 months. We opened it after staff and the college community expressed interest in having a cafe on campus and in the library. No similar cafe exists elsewhere on campus.
- The Library has been doing this for five years. We were responding to need/requests from students.

Table 2 - 1   Percentage of Food Operations Run by Various Organizations

Who runs the library's food operations?	THE COLLEGE FOOD PLAN COMPANY	AN INDEPENDENT COMPANY	THE LIBRARY	SOME OTHER UNIT OF THE COLLEGE
	19.23%	30.77%	34.62%	15.38%

Table 2 - 2   Percentage of Food Operations Run by Various Organizations, Broken Out by Type of Library

TYPE OF LIBRARY	THE COLLEGE FOOD PLAN COMPANY	AN INDEPENDENT COMPANY	THE LIBRARY	SOME OTHER UNIT OF THE COLLEGE
College Library	40.00%	10.00%	40.00%	10.00%
Public Library	0.00%	46.67%	33.33%	20.00%

Table 2 - 3   Percentage of Food Operations Run by Various Organizations, Broken Out by Number of Annual Visitors to the Library

ANNUAL VISITORS TO THE LIBRARY	THE COLLEGE FOOD PLAN COMPANY	AN INDEPENDENT COMPANY	THE LIBRARY	SOME OTHER UNIT OF THE COLLEGE
100,000 or fewer	0.00%	0.00%	100.00%	0.00%
100,001 - 250,000	50.00%	16.67%	33.33%	0.00%
250,001 - 600,000	14.29%	28.57%	28.57%	28.57%
601,000 or more	12.50%	62.50%	0.00%	25.00%

CHAPTER 3: PROFITABILITY OF SPECIFIC MEALS

Table 3 - 1   Percentage of Each Meal Type that Generates the Most Income for
the Library Food Service Operations

Which of the following meal types generates the most income for the library food service operations?	BREAKFAST	LUNCH	DINNER	GENERAL SNACKS
	8.33%	20.83%	0.00%	70.83%

Table 3 - 2   Percentage of Each Meal Type that Generates the Most Income for
the Library Food Service Operations, Broken Out by Type of Library

TYPE OF LIBRARY	BREAKFAST	LUNCH	DINNER	GENERAL SNACKS
College Library	12.50%	12.50%	0.00%	75.00%
Public Library	6.25%	25.00%	0.00%	68.75%

Table 3 - 3   Percentage of Each Meal Type that Generates the Most Income for
the Library Food Service Operations, Broken Out by Number of Annual Visitors to
the Library

ANNUAL VISITORS TO THE LIBRARY	BREAKFAST	LUNCH	DINNER	GENERAL SNACKS
100,000 or fewer	0.00%	33.33%	0.00%	66.67%
100,001 - 250,000	0.00%	0.00%	0.00%	100.00%
250,001 - 600,000	16.67%	33.33%	0.00%	50.00%
601,000 or more	14.29%	28.57%	0.00%	57.14%

CHAPTER 4: PROFITABILITY OF SPECIFIC FOODS AND DRINKS

Table 4 - 1   Mean, Median, Minimum and Maximum of Percentage of Total Revenues of the Library Café or Restaurant are Accounted for by Sales of Coffee

Approximately what percentage of total revenues of the library café or restaurant are accounted for by sales of coffee?	MEAN	MEDIAN	MINIMUM	MAXIMUM
	38.45	32.50	0.00	100.00

Table 4 - 2   Mean, Median, Minimum and Maximum of Percentage of Total Revenues of the Library Café or Restaurant are Accounted for by Sales of Coffee, Broken Out by Type of Library

TYPE OF LIBRARY	MEAN	MEDIAN	MINIMUM	MAXIMUM
College Library	58.57	75.00	0.00	100.00
Public Library	27.62	10.00	0.00	100.00

Table 4 - 3   Mean, Median, Minimum and Maximum of Percentage of Total Revenues of the Library Café or Restaurant are Accounted for by Sales of Coffee, Broken Out by Number of Annual Visitors to the Library

ANNUAL VISITORS TO THE LIBRARY	MEAN	MEDIAN	MINIMUM	MAXIMUM
100,000 or fewer	60.00	100.00	0.00	100.00
100,001 - 250,000	26.50	2.00	0.00	80.00
250,001 - 600,000	53.00	40.00	30.00	100.00
601,000 or more	11.25	5.00	0.00	35.00

Table 4 - 4   Mean, Median, Minimum and Maximum of Percentage of Total Revenues of the Library Café or Restaurant are Accounted for by Sales of Salads

Approximately what percentage of total revenues of the library café or restaurant are accounted for by sales of salads?	MEAN	MEDIAN	MINIMUM	MAXIMUM
	4.50	0.00	0.00	30.00

Table 4 - 5   Mean, Median, Minimum and Maximum of Percentage of Total Revenues of the Library Café or Restaurant are Accounted for by Sales of Salads, Broken Out by Type of Library

TYPE OF LIBRARY	MEAN	MEDIAN	MINIMUM	MAXIMUM
College Library	3.33	0.00	0.00	10.00
Public Library	5.83	0.00	0.00	30.00

Table 4 - 6   Mean, Median, Minimum and Maximum of Percentage of Total Revenues of the Library Café or Restaurant are Accounted for by Sales of Salads, Broken Out by Number of Annual Visitors to the Library

ANNUAL VISITORS TO THE LIBRARY	MEAN	MEDIAN	MINIMUM	MAXIMUM
100,000 or fewer	0.00	0.00	0.00	0.00
100,001 - 250,000	0.00	0.00	0.00	0.00
250,001 - 600,000	0.00	0.00	0.00	0.00
601,000 or more	9.00	5.00	0.00	30.00

Table 4 - 7   Mean, Median, Minimum and Maximum of Percentage of Total Revenues of the Library Café or Restaurant are Accounted for by Sales of Yogurt

Approximately what percentage of total revenues of the library café or restaurant are accounted for by sales of yogurt?	MEAN	MEDIAN	MINIMUM	MAXIMUM
	0.91	0.00	0.00	5.00

Table 4 - 8   Mean, Median, Minimum and Maximum of Percentage of Total Revenues of the Library Café or Restaurant are Accounted for by Sales of Yogurt, Broken Out by Type of Library

TYPE OF LIBRARY	MEAN	MEDIAN	MINIMUM	MAXIMUM
100,000 or fewer	1.67	0.00	0.00	5.00
100,001 - 250,000	0.71	0.00	0.00	5.00

Table 4 - 9   Mean, Median, Minimum and Maximum of Percentage of Total Revenues of the Library Café or Restaurant are Accounted for by Sales of Yogurt, Broken Out by Number of Annual Visitors to the Library

ANNUAL VISITORS TO THE LIBRARY	MEAN	MEDIAN	MINIMUM	MAXIMUM
100,000 or fewer	0.00	0.00	0.00	0.00
100,001 - 250,000	0.00	0.00	0.00	0.00
250,001 - 600,000	0.00	0.00	0.00	0.00
601,000 or more	2.00	0.00	0.00	5.00

Table 4 - 10   Mean, Median, Minimum and Maximum of Percentage of Total Revenues of the Library Café or Restaurant are Accounted for by Sales of Fruit

Approximately what percentage of total revenues of the library café or restaurant are accounted for by sales of fruit?	MEAN	MEDIAN	MINIMUM	MAXIMUM
	1.42	0.00	0.00	5.00

Table 4 - 11   Mean, Median, Minimum and Maximum of Percentage of Total Revenues of the Library Café or Restaurant are Accounted for by Sales of Fruit, Broken Out by Type of Library

TYPE OF LIBRARY	MEAN	MEDIAN	MINIMUM	MAXIMUM
College Library	1.67	0.00	0.00	5.00
Public Library	1.50	0.00	0.00	5.00

Table 4 - 12   Mean, Median, Minimum and Maximum of Percentage of Total Revenues of the Library Café or Restaurant are Accounted for by Sales of Fruit, Broken Out by Broken Out by Number of Annual Visitors to the Library

ANNUAL VISITORS TO THE LIBRARY	MEAN	MEDIAN	MINIMUM	MAXIMUM
100,000 or fewer	0.00	0.00	0.00	0.00
100,001 - 250,000	0.00	0.00	0.00	0.00
250,001 - 600,000	1.00	1.00	0.00	2.00
601,000 or more	3.00	5.00	0.00	5.00

Table 4 - 13   Mean, Median, Minimum and Maximum of Percentage of Total Revenues of the Library Café or Restaurant are Accounted for by Sales of "Junk" Foods

Approximately what percentage of total revenues of the library café or restaurant are accounted for by sales of "junk" foods?	MEAN	MEDIAN	MINIMUM	MAXIMUM
	14.29	7.50	0.00	60.00

Table 4 - 14   Mean, Median, Minimum and Maximum of Percentage of Total Revenues of the Library Café or Restaurant are Accounted for by Sales of "Junk" Foods, Broken Out by Type of Library

TYPE OF LIBRARY	MEAN	MEDIAN	MINIMUM	MAXIMUM
College Library	10.00	10.00	0.00	20.00
Public Library	17.00	10.00	0.00	60.00

Table 4 - 15   Mean, Median, Minimum and Maximum of Percentage of Total Revenues of the Library Café or Restaurant are Accounted for by Sales of "Junk" Foods, Broken Out by Number of Annual Visitors to the Library

ANNUAL VISITORS TO THE LIBRARY	MEAN	MEDIAN	MINIMUM	MAXIMUM
100,000 or fewer	0.00	0.00	0.00	0.00
100,001 - 250,000	33.33	40.00	0.00	60.00
250,001 - 600,000	6.67	5.00	0.00	15.00
601,000 or more	13.33	12.50	0.00	30.00

Table 4 - 16   Mean, Median, Minimum and Maximum of Percentage of Total Revenues of the Library Café or Restaurant are Accounted for by Sales of Sandwiches

Approximately what percentage of total revenues of the library café or restaurant are accounted for by sales of sandwiches?	MEAN	MEDIAN	MINIMUM	MAXIMUM
	5.00	0.00	0.00	30.00

Table 4 - 17   Mean, Median, Minimum and Maximum of Percentage of Total Revenues of the Library Café or Restaurant are Accounted for by Sales of Sandwiches, Broken Out by Type of Library

TYPE OF LIBRARY	MEAN	MEDIAN	MINIMUM	MAXIMUM
College Library	6.67	0.00	0.00	20.00
Public Library	5.00	0.00	0.00	30.00

Table 4 - 18   Mean, Median, Minimum and Maximum of Percentage of Total Revenues of the Library Café or Restaurant are Accounted for by Sales of Sandwiches, Broken Out by Number of Annual Visitors to the Library

ANNUAL VISITORS TO THE LIBRARY	MEAN	MEDIAN	MINIMUM	MAXIMUM
100,000 or fewer	0.00	0.00	0.00	0.00
100,001 - 250,000	0.00	0.00	0.00	0.00
250,001 - 600,000	0.00	0.00	0.00	0.00
601,000 or more	11.00	5.00	0.00	30.00

Table 4 - 19   Mean, Median, Minimum and Maximum of Percentage of Total Revenues of the Library Café or Restaurant are Accounted for by Sales of Cold Drinks

Approximately what percentage of total revenues of the library café or restaurant are accounted for by sales of cold drinks?	MEAN	MEDIAN	MINIMUM	MAXIMUM
	29.12	30.00	0.00	70.00

Table 4 - 20   Mean, Median, Minimum and Maximum of Percentage of Total Revenues of the Library Café or Restaurant are Accounted for by Sales of Cold Drinks, Broken Out by Type of Library

TYPE OF LIBRARY	MEAN	MEDIAN	MINIMUM	MAXIMUM
College Library	20.00	22.50	0.00	35.00
Public Library	31.92	30.00	0.00	70.00

Table 4 - 21   Mean, Median, Minimum and Maximum of Percentage of Total Revenues of the Library Café or Restaurant are Accounted for by Sales of Cold Drinks, Broken Out by Number of Annual Visitors to the Library

ANNUAL VISITORS TO THE LIBRARY	MEAN	MEDIAN	MINIMUM	MAXIMUM
100,000 or fewer	0.00	0.00	0.00	0.00
100,001 - 250,000	25.00	15.00	0.00	60.00
250,001 - 600,000	36.00	30.00	0.00	65.00
601,000 or more	38.00	35.00	15.00	70.00

Table 4 - 22   Mean, Median, Minimum and Maximum of Percentage of Total Revenues of the Library Café or Restaurant are Accounted for by Sales of Bakery Items

Approximately what percentage of total revenues of the library café or restaurant are accounted for by sales of bakery items?	MEAN	MEDIAN	MINIMUM	MAXIMUM
	7.20	5.00	0.00	28.00

Table 4 - 23   Mean, Median, Minimum and Maximum of Percentage of Total Revenues of the Library Café or Restaurant are Accounted for by Sales of Bakery Items, Broken Out by Type of Library

TYPE OF LIBRARY	MEAN	MEDIAN	MINIMUM	MAXIMUM
College Library	10.00	10.00	0.00	20.00
Public Library	6.18	0.00	0.00	28.00

Table 4 - 24   Mean, Median, Minimum and Maximum of Percentage of Total Revenues of the Library Café or Restaurant are Accounted for by Sales of Bakery Items, Broken Out by Number of Annual Visitors to the Library

ANNUAL VISITORS TO THE LIBRARY	MEAN	MEDIAN	MINIMUM	MAXIMUM
100,000 or fewer	0.00	0.00	0.00	0.00
100,001 - 250,000	5.00	5.00	0.00	10.00
250,001 - 600,000	11.00	5.00	0.00	28.00
601,000 or more	11.00	10.00	0.00	20.00

Table 4 - 25   Mean, Median, Minimum and Maximum of the Average Price of a Medium-Sized Cup of Coffee Sold in Library Café or Restaurant

What was the average price of a medium-sized cup of coffee sold in your library café or restaurant?	MEAN	MEDIAN	MINIMUM	MAXIMUM
	1.49	1.50	0.00	2.75

Table 4 - 26   Mean, Median, Minimum and Maximum of the Average Price of a Medium-Sized Cup of Coffee Sold in Library Café or Restaurant, Broken Out by Type of Library

TYPE OF LIBRARY	MEAN	MEDIAN	MINIMUM	MAXIMUM
College Library	1.38	1.59	0.50	2.00
Public Library	1.53	1.45	0.00	2.75

Table 4 - 27   Mean, Median, Minimum and Maximum of the Average Price of a Medium-Sized Cup of Coffee Sold in Library Café or Restaurant, Broken Out by Number of Annual Visitors to the Library

ANNUAL VISITORS TO THE LIBRARY	MEAN	MEDIAN	MINIMUM	MAXIMUM
100,000 or fewer	0.55	0.55	0.50	0.60
100,001 - 250,000	1.54	1.70	0.00	2.50
250,001 - 600,000	1.89	1.65	1.45	2.75
601,000 or more	1.60	1.50	1.25	2.50

Libraries' Best Selling Food Products

By far, the most popular foods items reported were from the "carb" family – muffins, scones, pastries, cookies, and crackers. Sandwiches, croissant sandwiches, wraps, pitas, salads, and soups were also mentioned; along with candy, chips, and other dessert items.

As you might expect, many libraries reported the traditional drink choices of coffee, tea, cocoa, soda, and other cold drinks as big sellers. A few reported more "upscale" expresso-based coffee drinks (lattes, etc.) and/or fruit-based drinks (smoothies) as popular choices.

- Smoothies, muffins, cookies
- Iced coffee drinks such as lattes.
- scones, cookies
- outsourced
- Cookies, scones, danish, cold drinks, coffee drinks, cocoa
- muffins
- only sell coffee
- we only sell pastries.
- muffins & other pastries from LOCAL bakery; small packages of crackers (goldfish) for young children.
- We are not progressive at all with our coffee & tea corner. We offer everything for free-- nuts & crackers, sometimes. At times the peppermints.
- candy
- We make the coffee and we do not charge for it. The only rule: if you got the last cup you have to make the next pot. We also have a one-cupper to heat water if you want tea
- Sandwiches, Wraps, Soups, Salads
- muffins, scones,italian sodas, cookies, crackers
- pastries
- coffee (no food items sold, or allowed, outside of vending area)
- sodas and chips
- espresso-based coffee drinks -- winter blended fruit drinks (smoothies) -- summer
- Sandwiches, chips and cookies
- Croissant sandwiches, signature salads, daily coffee, catered items, desserts
- Cookies, candy bars
- We only provide coffee and hot tea.
- Lunch menu items - sandwiches, pitas and salads.
- espresso drinks smoothies pastries cookies

- muffins, cookies

Libraries' Slowest Moving Products

Approximately half of the participants reported slow moving products. A disparate group of items was reported - hot dogs, sandwiches, fruit, yogurt, pastries, beef jerky, popcorn, and gum. Each item was reported only once, except for pastries, which was reported twice. Note that two items of the group – sandwiches and pastries – were also reported as best selling products.

- Sweet rolls; hot dogs
- not determined at this time
- outsourced
- only sell coffee
- fruit - gets old before it sells
- gum
- beef jerky
- large pastries
- popcorn, yogurt
- sandwiches

CHAPTER 5: STAFFING OF FOOD SERVICE OPERATIONS

Table 5 - 1   Mean, Median, Minimum and Maximum of Number of Full Time Positions, (Measured as FTE's) Accounted For by Positions in Library Café or Other Library Food Service Operations

How many full time positions (measured as FTE's) are accounted for by positions in the library café or other library food service operations?	MEAN	MEDIAN	MINIMUM	MAXIMUM
	1.17	0.00	0.00	7.00

Table 5 - 2   Mean, Median, Minimum and Maximum of Number of Full Time Positions, (Measured as FTE's) Accounted For by Positions in Library Café or Other Library Food Service Operations, Broken Out by Type of Library

TYPE OF LIBRARY	MEAN	MEDIAN	MINIMUM	MAXIMUM
College Library	1.17	0.00	0.00	4.00
Public Library	1.17	0.05	0.00	7.00

Table 5 - 3   Mean, Median, Minimum and Maximum of Number of Full Time Positions, (Measured as FTE's) Accounted For by Positions in Library Café or Other Library Food Service Operations, Broken Out by Number of Annual Visitors to the Library

ANNUAL VISITORS TO THE LIBRARY	MEAN	MEDIAN	MINIMUM	MAXIMUM
100,000 or fewer	0.17	0.00	0.00	1.00
100,001 - 250,000	0.77	0.80	0.00	1.50
250,001 - 600,000	1.50	1.00	0.00	4.00
601,000 or more	2.33	1.50	0.00	7.00

Table 5 - 4   Mean, Median, Minimum and Maximum of the Total Annual Cost of Salaries of Employees Who Work in the Café or Restaurant

Approximately what is the total annual cost of salaries of the employees who work in the café or restaurant?	MEAN	MEDIAN	MINIMUM	MAXIMUM
	13,320.00	0.00	0.00	115,500.00

Table 5 - 5   Mean, Median, Minimum and Maximum of the Total Annual Cost of Salaries of Employees Who Work in the Café or Restaurant, Broken Out by Type of Library

TYPE OF LIBRARY	MEAN	MEDIAN	MINIMUM	MAXIMUM
College Library	7,400.00	0.00	0.00	38,400.00
Public Library	15,857.14	0.00	0.00	115,500.00

Table 5 - 6   Mean, Median, Minimum and Maximum of the Total Annual Cost of Salaries of Employees Who Work in the Café or Restaurant, Broken Out by Number of Annual Visitors to the Library

ANNUAL VISITORS TO THE LIBRARY	MEAN	MEDIAN	MINIMUM	MAXIMUM
100,000 or fewer	1,000.00	0.00	0.00	6,000.00
100,001 - 250,000	5,500.00	1,000.00	0.00	20,000.00
250,001 - 600,000	16,900.00	0.00	0.00	84,500.00
601,000 or more	51,300.00	38,400.00	0.00	115,500.00

CHAPTER 6: HOURS OF OPERATION

School Year Operating Hours of Cafes or Restaurants

Library cafés and restaurants open as early as 7 AM and close as late as 10 PM during the school year.   Mostly the hours of operation parallel those of the library but there are differences. The list below relates the hours that the library cafes in the sample were open to the public.

- 7 a.m. - 10 p.m. M-Th, Friday 7 a.m. - 2 p.m., Sunday 4 p.m. - 10 p.m.
- 730AM-- 900PM
- same as library
- M-Th 9A-7:30P; F-Sa 10A-5:30P; Su 1P-4:30P
- 9 am to 8 pm
- public library hours 49 hrs/wk
- It is open regular library hours M-TH 10-9, Fri and Sat 10-5, Sunday 1-5 and they are open for some of the special events in evenings.
- 9am - 6 pm
- 8 am - 5 pm
- 7:30am-8:00pm
- 10:00 a.m.-4:00 p.m.
- 8-4:30
- 8:30am to 5:00pm
- 10am to 4pm Mon-Sat
- 8:a.m. to 9 p.m.
- 8am-8pm
- 7:45-3 & 6:30-8:30
- 8:15 am - 5:30 pm Monday-Friday, 9:00-5:00 Saturday, Sunday closed
- 10am to 5pm
- coffee is provided on weekday mornings
- 8 a.m. - 4 p.m.
- M-Th: 7 am-9 pm; F 7 am-4:30 pm
- 8am to 7pm

Summer Operating Hours of Cafes or Restaurants

Library cafés and restaurants open as early as 7 AM and close as late as 9 PM during the summer months.

- M-F 10 a.m. - 2 p.m.
- 800AM--500PM
- same as library
- M-Th 9A-7:30P; F-Sa 10A-5:30P; Su 1P-4:30P
- 9 am to 8 pm
- public library hours 49 hrs/wk
- Same except no Sundays
- 9 am - 6 pm
- 8 am - 5 pm
- not open in summer

- same, 10:00 a.m. - 4:00 p.m.
- 8-4:30
- 8:30am to 5:00pm
- 10am to 4pm Mon-Sat
- 8:a.m. to 9 p.m.
- 8am-8pm
- closed in summer
- 8:15 am - 5:30 pm Monday-Friday, 9:00-5:00 Saturday, Sunday closed
- 10am to 5pm
- weekday mornings
- 8 a.m. - 4 p.m.
- M-Th: 7 am-9 pm; F 7 am-4:30 pm; Sa 8 am-2 pm; Su 12 pm-6 pm
- 8am to 3pm, M - Thursday

CHAPTER 7: EFFECT OF FOOD SERVICE OPERATIONS ON OPERATING COSTS

Table 7 - 1   Percentage of Libraries Where Offering Food in the Library has Led to Higher Library Maintenance and Clean-Up Costs

Has offering food in the library led to higher library maintenance and clean up costs?	YES	NO
	22.58%	77.42%

Table 7 - 2   Percentage of Libraries Where Offering Food in the Library has Led to Higher Library Maintenance and Clean-Up Costs, Broken Out by Type of Library

TYPE OF LIBRARY	YES	NO
College Library	10.00%	90.00%
Public Library	25.00%	75.00%

Table 7 - 3   Percentage of Libraries Where Offering Food in the Library has Led to Higher Library Maintenance and Clean-Up Costs, Broken Out by Number of Annual Visitors to the Library

ANNUAL VISITORS TO THE LIBRARY	YES	NO
100,000 or fewer	0.00%	100.00%
100,001 - 250,000	37.50%	62.50%
250,001 - 600,000	12.50%	87.50%
601,000 or more	33.33%	66.67%

Table 7 - 4   Percentage of Libraries Where Offering Food in the Library has Led to Higher Carpeting, Furnishing or other Décor-Related Costs

Has offering food in the library led to higher Carpeting, Furnishing or other Décor-Related Costs?	YES	NO
	15.63%	84.38%

Table 7 - 5   Percentage of Libraries Where Offering Food in the Library has Led to Higher Carpeting, Furnishing or other Décor-Related Costs, Broken Out by Type of Library

TYPE OF LIBRARY	YES	NO
College Library	18.18%	81.82%
Public Library	10.00%	90.00%

Table 7 - 6   Percentage of Libraries Where Offering Food in the Library has Led to Higher Carpeting, Furnishing or other Décor-Related Costs, Broken Out by Number of Annual Visitors to the Library

ANNUAL VISITORS TO THE LIBRARY	YES	NO
100,000 or fewer	20.00%	80.00%
100,001 - 250,000	12.50%	87.50%
250,001 - 600,000	12.50%	87.50%
601,000 or more	22.22%	77.78%

Library Policies For Preventing Food Damage to Library Assets

We asked the libraries in the sample to briefly tell us what they did to prevent food and beverages from damaging library assets. Their responses are listed below:

- Lots of trash cans, requiring lids on drinks. The computer lab in the library does not allow food or drink.
- Food is contained in one area
- Policies indicate patron will be responsible for damages.
- None, other than advising caution.
- All drinks must be covered. Food is only permitted in the meeting and study rooms. No drinks by the computers
- Food and non-alcoholic beverages with lids are permitted in the cafe and throughout the library.
- Scotch guarding furniture
- Requesting patrons keep all food items in the cafe or foyer area of library
- The coffee shop is located in the lobby, before you get to the library. No food is allowed in the library only drinks with covered lids. We have had some spills but it has only been two months.
- No special measures, just have signs requesting patrons to let us know about spills so we can clean them up
- We just ask people to keep drinks away from computers.
- The only time that food is in the library is when staff has something to share, when story time leader has snacks for the children and when the Library Board has a special activity.
- all containers must have lids
- No policy. Food and drink are welcome anywhere in the library.
- The cafe is run by the Friends of the Library, strictly volunteers. The floor of the cafe space is slate, and volunteers continually tell people they cannot take food from cafe into the library. No library owned computers are in the cafe area. Public who come in through our front doors with their own food are invited to consume it in the Cafe space, a walk path from front to cafe, also a sealed slate floor. Cafe also is adjacent to public meeting rooms.
- All beverages must be in closed containers. No crumbly, greasy foods.
- The libraries have incurred minimal clean-up costs as a result of having food. In our meeting room policy we have a requirement for restoring the cleanliness of the meeting room. Though we allow food throughout the libraries, we do not have any other policies referring to food.
- Patrons pay for damage if it cannot be cleaned by maintenance
- Food is discouraged near the computers. No other policies (besides common courtesy) in place.
- We restrict food to the cafe area.
- Eat gently: what you drop today, you might sit in tomorrow.

- Food is not allowed out of the Cafe
- Cafe food and beverages are confined to a separate space w/ tables and chairs and tile floor.
- Food is allowed throughout the library except in the computer lab and the adult reading room.
- Beverages allowed in lidded/closed containers only
- Only drinks with lids are allowed in the library. All other food must be eaten in the courtyard around the cafe.
- Food is to be kept in the cafe area only.
- Drinks must be covered.
- We provide ample waste containers in study rooms and throughout. We have not found that there is much of a problem. In fact, we had more issues in the old building when we discouraged food and students would hide with it.
- Drinks with lids
- Food is to be consumed in the food area only and it is tiled.
- We ask patrons to keep beverages in the Atrium, unless they have a lid. If they have a lid, they can go nearly everywhere in the building.
- Food service area is in a building housing the used bookstore, art galleries and meeting space.
- Only covered beverages are allowed outside of the cafe in the library. No food is allowed in the library outside of the cafe.
- Just hope that everyone will clean up after themselves.

CHAPTER 8: SPECIAL AMENITIES IN LIBRARAY CAFÉS AND RESTAURANTS

Table 8 - 1   Percentage of Library Cafes or Restaurants that are Wireless Hot Spots

Is the library café or restaurant a wireless hot spot?	YES	NO
	90.00%	10.00%

Table 8 - 2   Percentage of Library Cafes or Restaurants that Are Wireless Hot Spots, Broken Out by Type of Library

TYPE OF LIBRARY	YES	NO
College Library	100.00%	0.00%
Public Library	83.33%	16.67%

Table 8 - 3   Percentage of Library Cafes or Restaurants that are Wireless Hot Spots, Broken Out by Number of Annual Visitors to the Library

ANNUAL VISITORS TO THE LIBRARY	YES	NO
100,000 or fewer	100.00%	0.00%
100,001 - 250,000	85.71%	14.29%
250,001 - 600,000	85.71%	14.29%
601,000 or more	88.89%	11.11%

Table 8 - 4   Percentage of Library Cafes or Restaurants that Offer Workstations to Students

Does the library café or restaurant offer workstations to students?	YES	NO
	25.00%	75.00%

Table 8 - 5   Percentage of Library Cafes or Restaurants that Offer Workstations to Students, Broken Out by Type of Library

TYPE OF LIBRARY	YES	NO
College Library	41.67%	58.33%
Public Library	15.79%	84.21%

Table 8 - 6   Percentage of Library Cafes or Restaurants that Offer Workstations to Students, Broken Out by Annual Visitors to the Library

ANNUAL VISITORS TO THE LIBRARY	YES	NO
100,000 or fewer	50.00%	50.00%
100,001 - 250,000	14.29%	85.71%
250,001 - 600,000	37.50%	62.50%
601,000 or more	11.11%	88.89%

Table 8 - 7   Percentage of Library Cafes or Restaurants that Offer Outdoor Seating

Does the library café or restaurant offer outdoor seating?	YES	NO
	40.63%	59.38%

Table 8 - 8   Percentage of Library Cafes or Restaurants that Offer Outdoor Seating, Broken Out by Type of Library

TYPE OF LIBRARY	YES	NO
College Library	25.00%	75.00%
Public Library	47.37%	52.63%

Table 8 - 9   Percentage of Library Cafes or Restaurants that Offer Outdoor Seating, Broken Out by Number of Annual Visitors to the Library

ANNUAL VISITORS TO THE LIBRARY	YES	NO
100,000 or fewer	16.67%	83.33%
100,001 - 250,000	28.57%	71.43%
250,001 - 600,000	62.50%	37.50%
601,000 or more	44.44%	55.56%

CHAPTER 9: SPECIFIC FOOD ITEMS SERVED

Table 9 - 1   Percentage of Library Cafés or Restaurants that Serve Muffins

Does your library cafe or restaurant serve muffins?	YES	NO
	51.28%	48.72%

Table 9 - 2   Percentage of Library Cafés or Restaurants that Serve Muffins, Broken Out by Type of Library

TYPE OF LIBRARY	YES	NO
College Library	46.15%	53.85%
Public Library	52.00%	48.00%

Table 9 - 3   Percentage of Library Cafés or Restaurants that Serve Muffins, Broken Out by Number of Annual Visitors to the Library

ANNUAL VISITORS TO THE LIBRARY	YES	NO
100,000 or fewer	0.00%	100.00%
100,001 - 250,000	55.56%	44.44%
250,001 - 600,000	62.50%	37.50%
601,000 or more	90.00%	10.00%

Table 9 - 4   Percentage of Library Cafés or Restaurants that Serve Croissants

Does your library cafe or restaurant serve croissants?	YES	NO
	30.77%	69.23%

Table 9 - 5   Percentage of Library Cafés or Restaurants that Serve Croissants, Broken Out by Type of Library

TYPE OF LIBRARY	YES	NO
College Library	30.77%	69.23%
Public Library	32.00%	68.00%

Table 9 - 6   Percentage of Library Cafés or Restaurants that Serve Croissants, Broken Out by Annual Visitors to the Library

ANNUAL VISITORS TO THE LIBRARY	YES	NO
100,000 or fewer	0.00%	100.00%
100,001 - 250,000	44.44%	55.56%
250,001 - 600,000	37.50%	62.50%
601,000 or more	50.00%	50.00%

Table 9 - 7   Percentage of Library Cafés or Restaurants that Serve Bagels

Does your library cafe or restaurant serve bagels?	YES	NO
	35.90%	64.10%

Table 9 - 8   Percentage of Library Cafés or Restaurants that Serve Bagels, Broken Out by Type of Library

TYPE OF LIBRARY	YES	NO
College Library	30.77%	69.23%
Public Library	40.00%	60.00%

Table 9 - 9   Percentage of Library Cafés or Restaurants that Serve Bagels, Broken Out by Number of Annual Visitors to the Library

ANNUAL VISITORS TO THE LIBRARY	YES	NO
100,000 or fewer	0.00%	100.00%
100,001 - 250,000	44.44%	55.56%
250,001 - 600,000	50.00%	50.00%
601,000 or more	60.00%	40.00%

Table 9 - 10   Percentage of Library Cafés or Restaurants that Serve Sandwiches

Does your library cafe or restaurant serve sandwiches?	YES	NO
	28.21%	71.79%

Table 9 - 11   Percentage of Library Cafés or Restaurants that Serve Sandwiches, Broken Out by Type of Library

TYPE OF LIBRARY	YES	NO
College Library	30.77%	69.23%
Public Library	28.00%	72.00%

Table 9 - 12   Percentage of Library Cafés or Restaurants that Serve Sandwiches, Broken Out by Number of Annual Visitors to the Library

ANNUAL VISITORS TO THE LIBRARY	YES	NO
100,000 or fewer	0.00%	100.00%
100,001 - 250,000	33.33%	66.67%
250,001 - 600,000	37.50%	62.50%
601,000 or more	50.00%	50.00%

Table 9 - 13   Percentage of Library Cafés or Restaurants that Serve Hot Sandwiches

Does your library cafe or restaurant serve hot sandwiches?	YES	NO
	12.82%	87.18%

Table 9 - 14   Percentage of Library Cafés or Restaurants that Serve Hot Sandwiches, Broken Out by Type of Library

TYPE OF LIBRARY	YES	NO
College Library	0.00%	100.00%
Public Library	20.00%	80.00%

Table 9 - 15   Percentage of Library Cafés or Restaurants that Serve Hot Sandwiches, Broken Out by Number of Annual Visitors to the Library

ANNUAL VISITORS TO THE LIBRARY	YES	NO
100,000 or fewer	0.00%	100.00%
100,001 - 250,000	0.00%	100.00%
250,001 - 600,000	25.00%	75.00%
601,000 or more	30.00%	70.00%

Table 9 - 16   Percentage of Library Cafés or Restaurants that Serve Grilled Sandwiches

Does your library cafe or restaurant serve grilled sandwiches?	YES	NO
	12.82%	87.18%

Table 9 - 17   Percentage of Library Cafés or Restaurants that Serve Grilled Sandwiches, Broken Out by Type of Library

TYPE OF LIBRARY	YES	NO
College Library	0.00%	100.00%
Public Library	20.00%	80.00%

Table 9 - 18   Percentage of Library Cafés or Restaurants that Serve Grilled Sandwiches, Broken Out by Number of Annual Visitors to the Library

ANNUAL VISITORS TO THE LIBRARY	YES	NO
100,000 or fewer	0.00%	100.00%
100,001 - 250,000	0.00%	100.00%
250,001 - 600,000	25.00%	75.00%
601,000 or more	30.00%	70.00%

Table 9 - 19   Percentage of Library Cafés or Restaurants that Serve Hamburgers

Does your library cafe or restaurant serve hamburgers?	YES	NO
	5.13%	94.87%

Table 9 - 20   Percentage of Library Cafés or Restaurants that Serve Hamburgers, Broken Out by Type of Library

TYPE OF LIBRARY	YES	NO
College Library	0.00%	100.00%
Public Library	8.00%	92.00%

Table 9 - 21   Percentage of Library Cafés or Restaurants that Serve Hamburgers, Broken Out by Number of Annual Visitors to the Library

ANNUAL VISITORS TO THE LIBRARY	YES	NO
100,000 or fewer	0.00%	100.00%
100,001 - 250,000	0.00%	100.00%
250,001 - 600,000	0.00%	100.00%
601,000 or more	20.00%	80.00%

Table 9 - 22   Percentage of Library Cafés or Restaurants that Serve Soup

Does your library cafe or restaurant serve soup?	YES	NO
	17.95%	82.05%

Table 9 - 23   Percentage of Library Cafés or Restaurants that Serve Soup, Broken Out by Type of Library

TYPE OF LIBRARY	YES	NO
College Library	7.69%	92.31%
Public Library	24.00%	76.00%

Table 9 - 24   Percentage of Library Cafés or Restaurants that Serve Soup, Broken Out by Number of Annual Visitors to the Library

ANNUAL VISITORS TO THE LIBRARY	YES	NO
100,000 or fewer	0.00%	100.00%
100,001 - 250,000	22.22%	77.78%
250,001 - 600,000	25.00%	75.00%
601,000 or more	30.00%	70.00%

Table 9 - 25   Percentage of Library Cafés or Restaurants Food Service Operations that Serve Main Entrees

Does your library cafe or restaurant serve main entrees?	YES	NO
	5.13%	94.87%

Table 9 - 26   Percentage of Library Cafés or Restaurants that Serve Main Entrees, Broken Out by Type of Library

TYPE OF LIBRARY	YES	NO
College Library	0.00%	100.00%
Public Library	8.00%	92.00%

Table 9 - 27   Percentage of Library Cafés or Restaurants that Serve Main Entrees, Broken Out by Number of Annual Visitors to the Library

ANNUAL VISITORS TO THE LIBRARY	YES	NO
100,000 or fewer	0.00%	100.00%
100,001 - 250,000	0.00%	100.00%
250,001 - 600,000	0.00%	100.00%
601,000 or more	20.00%	80.00%

Table 9 - 28   Percentage of Library Cafés or Restaurants that Serve Yogurt

Does your library cafe or restaurant serve yogurt?	YES	NO
	20.51%	79.49%

Table 9 - 29   Percentage of Library Cafés or Restaurants that Serve Yogurt, Broken Out by Type of Library

TYPE OF LIBRARY	YES	NO
College Library	23.08%	76.92%
Public Library	20.00%	80.00%

Table 9 - 30   Percentage of Library Cafés or Restaurants that Serve Yogurt, Broken Out by Number of Annual Visitors to the Library

ANNUAL VISITORS TO THE LIBRARY	YES	NO
100,000 or fewer	0.00%	100.00%
100,001 - 250,000	22.22%	77.78%
250,001 - 600,000	12.50%	87.50%
601,000 or more	50.00%	50.00%

Table 9 - 31   Percentage of Library Cafés or Restaurants that Serve Popcorn

Does your library cafe or restaurant serve popcorn?	YES	NO
	5.13%	94.87%

Table 9 - 32   Percentage of Library Cafés or Restaurants that Serve Popcorn, Broken Out by Type of Library

TYPE OF LIBRARY	YES	NO
College Library	0.00%	100.00%
Public Library	8.00%	92.00%

Table 9 - 33   Percentage of Library Cafés or Restaurants that Serve Popcorn, Broken Out by Number of Annual Visitors to the Library

ANNUAL VISITORS TO THE LIBRARY	YES	NO
100,000 or fewer	0.00%	100.00%
100,001 - 250,000	0.00%	100.00%
250,001 - 600,000	0.00%	100.00%
601,000 or more	20.00%	80.00%

CHAPTER 10: EFFECT OF CAFES AND RESTAURANTS ON LIBRARY VISITATION

Table 10 - 1   Percentage of Library Cafés or Restaurants that Have Been Successful in Increasing the Number of Patrons Visiting the Library

Has your library café or restaurant been successful in increasing the number of patrons who visit the library?	YES	NO
	65.52%	34.48%

Table 10 - 2   Percentage of Library Cafés or Restaurants that Have Been Successful in Increasing the Number of Patrons Visiting the Library, Broken Out by Type of Library

TYPE OF LIBRARY	YES	NO
College Library	72.73%	27.27%
Public Library	58.82%	41.18%

Table 10 - 3   Percentage of Library Cafés or Restaurants that Have Been Successful in Increasing the Number of Patrons Visiting the Library, Broken Out by Number of Annual Visitors to the Library

ANNUAL VISITORS TO THE LIBRARY	YES	NO
100,000 or fewer	60.00%	40.00%
100,001 - 250,000	66.67%	33.33%
250,001 - 600,000	87.50%	12.50%
601,000 or more	62.50%	37.50%

Table 10 - 4   Percentage of Libraries for Whom Operating a Café in the Library has Led Patrons to Spend More Time in the Library

Has operating a café in the library led to patrons spending more time in the library?	YES	NO
	89.66%	10.34%

Table 10 - 5   Percentage of Libraries for Whom Operating a Café in the Library has Led Patrons to Spend More Time in the Library, Broken Out by Type of Library

TYPE OF LIBRARY	YES	NO
College Library	72.73%	27.27%
Public Library	100.00%	0.00%

Table 10 - 6   Percentage of Libraries for Whom Operating a Café in the Library has Led Patrons to Spend More Time in the Library, Broken Out by Number of Annual Visitors to the Library

ANNUAL VISITORS TO THE LIBRARY	YES	NO
100,000 or fewer	40.00%	60.00%
100,001 - 250,000	100.00%	0.00%
250,001 - 600,000	100.00%	0.00%
601,000 or more	100.00%	0.00%

CHAPTER 11: USE OF VENDING MACHINES, MOBILE KIOSKS, AND CARTS

Table 11 - 1   Percentage of Libraries that Have Vending Machines in Any of Their Buildings

Does the library have vending machines in any of its buildings?	YES	NO
	64.71%	35.29%

Table 11 - 2   Percentage of Libraries that Have Vending Machines in Any of Their Buildings, Broken Out by Type of Library

TYPE OF LIBRARY	YES	NO
College Library	63.64%	36.36%
Public Library	63.64%	36.36%

Table 11 - 3   Percentage of Libraries that Have Vending Machines in Any of Their Buildings, Broken Out by Number of Annual Visitors to the Library

ANNUAL VISITORS TO THE LIBRARY	YES	NO
100,000 or fewer	42.86%	57.14%
100,001 - 250,000	71.43%	28.57%
250,001 - 600,000	62.50%	37.50%
601,000 or more	80.00%	20.00%

Table 11 - 4   Mean, Median, Minimum and Maximum of the Number of Vending Machines Libraries Have In All of Their Locations and Buildings

How many vending machines does the library have in all its locations and buildings?	MEAN	MEDIAN	MINIMUM	MAXIMUM
	2.96	2.00	0.00	12.00

Table 11 - 5   Mean, Median, Minimum and Maximum of the Number of Vending Machines Libraries Have In All of Their Locations and Buildings, Broken Out by Type of Library

TYPE OF LIBRARY	MEAN	MEDIAN	MINIMUM	MAXIMUM
College Library	3.00	3.00	0.00	6.00
Public Library	3.00	2.00	0.00	12.00

Table 11 - 6   Mean, Median, Minimum and Maximum of the Number of Vending Machines Libraries Have In All of Their Locations and Buildings, Broken Out by Number of Annual Visitors to the Library

ANNUAL VISITORS TO THE LIBRARY	MEAN	MEDIAN	MINIMUM	MAXIMUM
100,000 or fewer	1.40	1.00	0.00	3.00
100,001 - 250,000	2.33	2.00	0.00	6.00
250,001 - 600,000	3.50	2.00	0.00	12.00
601,000 or more	4.14	4.00	1.00	7.00

Table 11 - 7   Percentage of Libraries that Have Mobile Kiosks or Carts to Serve Out of the Way Places in the Library

Does the library have mobile kiosks or carts to serve out of the way places in the library?	YES	NO
	0.00%	100.00%

Table 11 - 8   Percentage of Libraries that Have Mobile Kiosks or Carts to Serve Out of the Way Places in the Library, Broken Out by Type of Library

TYPE OF LIBRARY	YES	NO
College Library	0.00%	100.00%
Public Library	0.00%	100.00%

Table 11 - 9   Percentage of Libraries that Have Mobile Kiosks or Carts to Serve Out of the Way Places in the Library, Broken Out by Number of Annual Visitors to the Library

ANNUAL VISITORS TO THE LIBRARY	YES	NO
100,000 or fewer	0.00%	100.00%
100,001 - 250,000	0.00%	100.00%
250,001 - 600,000	0.00%	100.00%
601,000 or more	0.00%	100.00%

CHAPTER 12: THE LIBRARY CAFÉ OR RESTAURANT AS A CATERER

Table 12 - 1   Percentage of Library Cafes or Restaurants that Cater Library Functions

Does the library café or restaurant do catering of library functions?	YES	NO
	34.38%	65.63%

Table 12 - 2   Percentage of Library Cafes or Restaurants that Cater Library Functions, Broken Out by Type of Library

TYPE OF LIBRARY	YES	NO
College Library	9.09%	90.91%
Public Library	50.00%	50.00%

Table 12 - 3   Percentage of Library Cafes or Restaurants that Cater Library Functions, Broken Out by Number of Annual Visitors to the Library

ANNUAL VISITORS TO THE LIBRARY	YES	NO
100,000 or fewer	0.00%	100.00%
100,001 - 250,000	28.57%	71.43%
250,001 - 600,000	42.86%	57.14%
601,000 or more	50.00%	50.00%

CHAPTER 13: ADVICE TO LIBRARIES ON STARTING A CAFE

Table 13 - 1   Percentage of Libraries Offering Various Kinds of Advice to Similarly Situated Libraries Wanting to Start a Library Cafe

What advice would you give to a library similar to your own that wanted to start a library café?	DON'T START ONE	START ONE AND HAVE A FRANCHISE RUN IT	START ONE AND HAVE THE LIBRARY RUN IT	START ONE AND HAVE THE COLLEGE FOOD SERVICE RUN IT
	6.45%	51.61%	16.13%	25.81%

Table 13 - 2   Percentage of Libraries Offering Various Kinds of Advice to Similarly Situated Libraries Wanting to Start a Library Cafe, Broken Out by Type of Library

TYPE OF LIBRARY	DON'T START ONE	START ONE AND HAVE A FRANCHISE RUN IT	START ONE AND HAVE THE LIBRARY RUN IT	START ONE AND HAVE THE COLLEGE FOOD SERVICE RUN IT
College Library	8.33%	25.00%	8.33%	58.33%
Public Library	5.56%	72.22%	22.22%	0.00%

Table 13 - 3   Percentage of Libraries Offering Various Kinds of Advice to Similarly Situated Libraries Wanting to Start a Library Cafe, Broken Out by Number of Annual Visitors to the Library

ANNUAL VISITORS TO THE LIBRARY	DON'T START ONE	START ONE AND HAVE A FRANCHISE RUN IT	START ONE AND HAVE THE LIBRARY RUN IT	START ONE AND HAVE THE COLLEGE FOOD SERVICE RUN IT
100,000 or fewer	16.67%	16.67%	16.67%	50.00%
100,001 - 250,000	0.00%	50.00%	12.50%	37.50%
250,001 - 600,000	16.67%	66.67%	16.67%	0.00%
601,000 or more	0.00%	55.56%	22.22%	22.22%

APPENDIX 1: Institutional Entity for Which Data was Supplied

We asked the libraries in the sample to specify the exact institutional entities for which they were supplying data. Their responses are listed below.

- Western Kentucky University has 3 libraries on the main campus, plus one library on a branch campus. These consist of the Helm-Cravens Library, which contains most of the materials; the Educational Resources Center; and the Kentucky Library & Museum, which is devoted to historical research and special collections. The cafe is located in the Helm-Cravens Library, which is the main library on the main campus.
- public library (sole location, no branches)
- main public library with one branch
- Main (and only) library.
- One public library
- Public Library: main library and 2 branch libraries to open coffee cafes in next year.
- Main public library - single location system
- Michener is one branch of 7 in Bucks County Free Library System, Pennsylvania - public library
- This data is for a single library location, the Joseph T. Simpson Public Library.
- I am only giving information for the Virginia Beach Central Library
- Only library for Barton
- One Public Library - no branches
- Small rural library with a town population of 2214.
- The Coffey County Library is a part of six branches. The visitors are many of the same people who are registered and therefore counted again and again.
- only library at Kansas City Kansas Community College
- We are a single library at a community college.
- Public Library. Annual budget for main and two branches. Cafe data for new main library only (open 5 months)
- giving data for all libraries and all cafes of MCC
- 9-library public library system (includes main library and all branch libraries)
- Academic library - one branch
- The only library on the campus of Brigham Young University-Idaho (not to be confused with our sister campus, BYU in Provo, Utah).
- The only library at Gogebic Community College
- We are part of the University Of Detroit Mercy Library system which consists of our library (Dental), the Kresge Law Library, and the McNichols Campus Library. Questions will be answered only for the Dental Library.
- Main Library Only regarding cafe service
- Main Public Library
- Main Library
- one building, main library
- Main Library is the only one with a cafe, so this data is for the Main Library only. We also have 3 branches.
- The cafe in Hernando Public Library a branch of First Regional Library
- Answering specifically for Germantown Public Library only.
- Main library & cafe (only one) at 4 year, very small, private university
- Main Public Library
- This data is for a library district with 12 branches. Two have eating locations, one a cafe

and one a vending machine area for the public.

- For our Main Library only.
- Cafe' is located at the Main Library of the Central Arkansas Library System, which has twelve branches.
- College of DuPage Library is the only library for the college, and the cafe is the only cafe in the library.
- All of the library locations, UT Arlington

OTHER REPORTS FROM PRIMARY RESEARCH GROUP, INC.

BEST PRACTICES OF PUBLIC LIBRARY INFORMATION TECHNOLOGY DIRECTORS
Price: $65.00   Publication Date: February 2005   ISBN: 1-57440-073-8

This special report is based on exhaustive interviews with information technology directors and other critical staff involved in IT decision-making from public libraries of Princeton, Evansville, San Francisco, Boston, Denver, Santa Monica, Columbus, Minneapolis, Cedar Falls and Seattle. The report – which is in an interview format and presents the views of the institutions cited above as well as Primary Research Group commentary – presents insights into the myriad of technology related issues confronting today's public librarians, including issues involved with: technology department staffing, internet filtering, workstation management and development, equipment and vendor selection, database licensing, internet access policies, automated book check in and check out systems, data back up, web site maintenance, cataloging, catalog enhancements, digitization of special collections, development of wireless access and other issues of interest to public librarians.

CREATING THE DIGITAL ART LIBRARY
Price: $80.00   Publication Date: October 2005   ISBN #: 1-57440-074-6

This special report looks at the efforts of ten leading art libraries and image collections to digitize their holdings. The study reports on the efforts of ARTstor, The National Gallery of Canada, Cornell University's Knight Resource Center, the University of North Carolina, Chapel Hill; the Smithsonian Institution Libraries, The Illinois Institute of Technology, The National Archives and Records Administration, McGill University, Ohio State University, the Cleveland Museum of Art, and the joint effort of Harvard, Princeton, The University of California, San Diego, the University of Minnesota and others to develop a union catalog for cultural objects.

Among the issues covered: cost of outsourcing, cost of in-house conversions, the future of 35 mm slides and related equipment, use of ARTstor and other commercial services, ease of interlibrary loan in images and the creation of a union catalog, prioritizing holdings for digitization, relationship of art libraries to departmental image collections, marketing image collections, range of end users of image collections, determining levels of access to the collection, digitization and distribution of backup materials on artists lives and times, equipment selection, copyright, and other issues in the creation and maintenance of digital art libraries.

The aim of the report is to impart practical advice from others who have already or are in the process of digitizing their collections.

TRENDS IN MANAGEMENT OF LIBRARY SPECIAL COLLECTIONS IN FILM & PHOTOGRAPHY
Price: $80.00   Publication Date: October 2005   ISBN #: 1-57440-075-4

This special report looks at the management and development of America's thriving special collections in film and photography. The report profiles the following collections: The University of Louisville, the Photographic Archives; the University of Utah's Multimedia Collection; The American Institute of Physics' Emilio Segre Visual Archives; The Newsfilm Library at the University of South Carolina; The University of California, Berkeley Pacific Film Archive; the UCLA Film and Television Archive, the Vanderbilt University Television News Archive; The

National Archives and Records Administration's Special Media Preservation Laboratory; and the University of Washington's Digital Initiatives Program.

The report covers digitization of photographs and film, special collection marketing, collection procurement, funding and financing, approaches for optimizing both sales revenues and educational uses, development of web-based sale and distribution systems for photography and film, systems to assure copyright compliance, the development of online searchable databases, and many other aspects of film and photography special collection management.

BEST PRACTICES OF ACADEMIC LIBRARY INFORMATION TECHNOLOGY DIRECTORS
Price: $75.00   Publication Date: February 25, 2005   ISBN: 1-57440-072-X

This study is based on interviews with IT directors and assistant directors of leading college and university libraries and consortiums, including The Research Libraries Group, Vanderbilt University, the University of Texas, Lewis & Clark College, Salt Lake Community College, the University of Washington, the California Institute of Technology, Hutchinson Community College and Australia's Monash University,

Among the many topics covered are: investment in and maintenance of workstations, implementation of wireless access, policies towards laptops in the library, digitizing special collections, establishing digital depositories, preserving scholarly access to potentially temporal digital media, use of Ebooks, services for distance learning students, use of url resolvers, web site development and management, use of virtual reference, investment in library software, IT staff size and staff skill composition, range of IT staff responsibilities, use of outsourcing, relations between Library and general University IT staff, uses of PHP programming, catalog integration with the web, catalog enhancement software and services, web site search engine policies, use of automated electronic collection management software, technology education and training, development of technology centers and information literacy, library printing technology and cost reimbursement, and other issues of concern to library information technology staff directors.

TRAINING COLLEGE STUDENTS IN INFORMATION LITERACY, 2006-07 EDITION
Publication Date: December 2006   Price: $69.50   ISBN: 1-57440-081-9

This report looks closely at emerging trends in information literacy training at the undergraduate and graduate levels in American higher education. The report includes profiles of information literacy efforts at Syracuse University, the University of Windsor, Ulster County Community College, The University of North Texas, the University of North Carolina at Chapel Hill, Indiana University, The University of California, Berkeley, USC, the University of Connecticut, Seattle Pacific University, NC State Wilmington, Southeastern Oklahoma State and others.

EMERGING ISSUES IN ACADEMIC LIBRARY CATALOGING & TECHNICAL SERVICES
ISBN: 1-57440-086-X   Price: $72.50   Publication Date: April 2007

This report presents nine highly detailed case studies of leading university cataloging and technical service departments. It provide insights into how they are handling ten major changes facing them, including: the encouragement of cataloging productivity; impact of new technologies and enhancement of online catalogs; transition to metadata standards; cataloging of websites and digital and other special collections; library catalog and metadata training; database maintenance, holdings, and physical processing; relationship with Acquisitions; staff education; and other important issues. Survey participants represent academic libraries of varying sizes and classifications, with many different viewpoints. Universities surveyed are: Brigham Young; Curry College; Haverford College; Illinois, Louisiana and Pennsylvania State Universities; University of North Dakota; University of Washington; and Yale.

PREVAILING & BEST PRACTICES IN ELECTRONIC AND PRINT SERIALS MANAGEMENT
Price: $80.00   Publication Date: November 2005   ISBN#: 1- 57440-076-2

This report looks closely at the electronic and print serials procurement and management practices of eleven libraries including: The University of Ohio, Villanova University; the Colorado School of Mines, Carleton College, Northwestern University; Baylor University, Princeton University, the University of Pennsylvania, the University of San Francisco, Embry-Riddle Aeronautical University and the University of Nebraska Medical Center. The report looks at both electronic and print serials and includes discussions of the following issues: selection and management of serials agents, including the negotiation of payment; allocating the serials budget by department; resolving access issues with publishers; use of consortiums in journal licensing; invoice reconciliation and payment; periodicals binding, claims, check in and management; serials department staff size and range of responsibilities; serials management software; use of open access archives and university depositories; policies on gift subscriptions, free trials and academic exchanges of publications; use of electronic serials/catalog linking technology; acquisition of usage statistics; cooperative arrangements with other local libraries and other issues in serials management.

THE SURVEY OF ACADEMIC LIBRARIES, 2006-07 Edition
Price $85.00   ISBN 1-57440-080-0

This survey presents detailed data from a survey of academic libraries with data broken out by size and type of library. The report presents more than 300 tables and charts about a myriad of library policy issues, such as number of grants received and applied for, time spent preparing grants, and the percentage of libraries with special collections in art, music, photography, film, rare books, and other areas. It includes detailed staffing and materials spending benchmarks, data on the development of library technology centers, and hard numbers about librarian time spent on information literacy. Also covered are policies on workstation development and the lending out of laptops, and many other aspects of academic librarianship.

THE SURVEY OF COLLEGE MARKETING PROGRAMS, 2007 Edition
Price: $295.00   Number of Tables: 600+   Pages: 164   Publication Date: December 2006
PDF: $320   College-Wide Site License: $395.00

This study is based on an exhaustive survey of 55 American colleges. Data is broken out by type of college, public or private status of the college, enrollment size, and extent of student body drawn from the local area. This exhaustive study presents highly detailed data on use of direct mail, viewbook publishing, college website development, radio and television advertising, newspaper advertising, web marketing and many other facets of college marketing.

Get the opinions of dozens of college marketing directors about a plethora of new strategies, tactics and options in college marketing. Find out what they think of emerging web marketing vehicles, how they are spending their marketing budgets, and what they have planned for the coming years.

The report gives hard data on the number and cost of viewbooks printed, spending on search engine placement and website ads, spending on market research and advertising consultants, staff time spent marketing through blogs, percentage of colleges that advertise in various types of newspapers and much much more.

THE SURVEY OF LAW FIRM eMARKETING PRACTICES
Price: $295.00   Number of Tables: 120+   Number of Questions 46   Number of Participants: 40

This study is based on a survey of 40 law firms with a mean size of 211 lawyers; data is broken out by size of law firm (by number of total lawyers) and by number of practice groups. Some data is also presented on a per partner basis, such as spending on website development, per partner. In each firm a major marketing official answered questions regarding editorial staff, website development and marketing, use of blogs, listservs, eNewsletters and other cyberspace promotion and information vehicles.

The report presents hard data on the use of search engine placement consultants, click through rates on eNewsletters, number of unique visitors to the firm website, and presents data on law firm spending plans for a broad range of Emarketing vehicles. The report presents hard data on law firm use of opt-in email, banner ads, website sponsorship, per click payments to Google, Yahoo, MSN and Overture, and much more.

The study also discusses the impact of web-based press release distribution services and presents data on the number of law firms that use, and plan to use such services. In addition to examining the prevailing methods of eMarketing, the report looks at law firm intentions in emerging eMarketing methods such as podcasting, webcasting and streaming video, among others. The report presents quantitative assessment data on the usefulness of specific online directory sites such as Law.com, Findlaw.com and Superpages.com. and others.

LAW LIBRARY BENCHMARKS, 2006-7 Edition
Price: $119.50 Publication Date: April 2006

Data broken out for law firm, university law school, and public sector law libraries. Some data is also broken out for corporate law departments. The report provides data from more than 80 major law libraries library and covers subjects such as staff size and growth, salaries and budget, spending trends in the library content budget, use of blogs, listservs and RSS feeds, spending on databases and commercial online services, use of and plans for CD-ROM,   parent organization management's view of the future of the law library, assessment of attorney search skills, trends in information literacy training, use of reference tracking software and much more.

LICENSING AND COPYRIGHT MANAGEMENT: BEST PRACTICES OF COLLEGE, SPECIAL, AND RESEARCH LIBRARIES
PRICE: $80   MAY 2004   ISBN: 1-57440-068-1

This report looks closely at the licensing and copyright-management strategies of a sample of leading research, college and special libraries and consortiums and includes interviews with leading experts. The focus is on electronic-database licensing, and includes discussions of the most pressing issues: development of consortiums and group buying initiatives, terms of access, liability for infringement, archiving, training and development, free-trial periods, contract language, contract-management software and time-management issues, acquiring and using usage statistics, elimination of duplication, enhancement of bargaining power, open-access publishing policies, interruption-of-service contingency arrangements, changes in pricing over the life of the contract, interlibrary loan of electronic files, copyright clearance, negotiating tactics, uses of consortiums, and many other issues. The report profiles the emergence of consortiums and group-buying arrangements.

CREATING THE DIGITAL ACADEMIC LIBRARY
Price: $69.50   JULY 2004   ISBN: 1-57440- 071-1

This report looks closely at the efforts of more than ten major academic libraries to develop their digital assets and deal with problems in the area of librarian time management, database selection, vendor relations, contract negotiation and tracking, electronic-resources funding and marketing, technical development, archival access, open access publishing agit prop, use of e-books, digitization of audio and image collections and other areas of the development of the digital academic library. The report includes profiles of Columbia University School of Medicine, the Health Sciences Complex of the University of Texas, Duke University Law Library, the University of Indiana Law Library, the University of South Carolina, the University of Idaho, and many others.

CREATING THE DIGITAL MEDICAL LIBRARY
Price: $ 99.50   Publication Date: June 2003 ISBN #: 1-57440-061-4

Creating the Digital Medical Library profiles the electronic collection development and electronic library development policies of a sample of leading medical libraries including those of the Mayo Clinic, Cornell University, the University of Iowa, Columbia University, the University of Texas, the Medical College of Georgia and many others.   The report covers policies concerning electronic journals, archiving, e-books, electronic directories, database user training, use of alert service, virtual reference services, negotiating tactics with vendors, sharing electronic resources with other libraries or a main campus library, electronic documents delivery, librarian time management, web site redevelopment and design, the impact of evidence-based medicine on library practices, employment of librarians on medical clinical teams, attitudes towards university-inspired or controlled   cooperative scholarly publishing ventures,   efforts to develop endowments/funds for digital resources,   cost control efforts, and other issues of concern to medical librarians. Also includes critical and recent benchmarking information on spending plans focusing primarily though not exclusively on digital resources.

CREATING THE DIGITAL LAW LIBRARY
Price: $95.00   Publication Date: June 2003   ISBN#: 1-57440-062-2

This report profiles digital library development policies of leading law libraries including those of Thompson Hine, Cassells Brock & Blackwell, Seyfarth Shaw, Ivins Phillips & Barker, Querrey @ Harrow, Lawrence County Law Library, Duke University Law Library, the University of Indiana Law Library, and others.   The report covers policies concerning electronic journals, archiving, e-books, electronic directories, database user training, use of alert service, virtual reference services, negotiating tactics with vendors, electronic documents delivery, librarian time management, web site redevelopment and design and other issues.

CREATING THE VIRTUAL REFERENCE SERVICE
ISBN 1-57440-058-4   Price: $85.00
Publication date: January 2003

This new report from Primary Research Group profiles the efforts of 15 academic, special and public libraries to develop digital reference services. The aim of the study is to enable other libraries to benefit from their experience in deciding whether and how to develop a digital reference service, how much time, money and other resources to spend on it, how to plan it, institute it and evaluate it. Let librarians - in their own words - tell you about their experiences with digital reference.

Among the libraries and other organizations profiled are: Pennsylvania State University, Syracuse University's Virtual Reference Desk, the Massachusetts Institute of Technology, Palomar College, The Library of Congress, the University of Florida, PA Librarian Live, the Douglas County Public Library, the Cleveland Public Library, Denver Public Library, OCLC, the New England Law Library Consortium, the Internet Public Library, Paradise Valley Community College, Yale University Law School, Oklahoma State University, Tutor.Com and Baruch College.

Some of the issues covered include: Email, phone, in-person and chat room reference query volume, software selection, software acquisition costs, software training, criteria for evaluation and success, monitoring usage, hours of service offered, demographics of usage, integration of digital reference with knowledge management programs, means of distributing queries to correct librarian, time demands on librarians, dealing with digital harassment, query answer time, use of direct links to reference librarian within library databases, marketing the digital reference service, real time vs email performance, use of publicly available services, participation in partnerships and cooperatives, impact on traditional reference services -- and many other issues and problems confronting the current or potential virtual librarian.